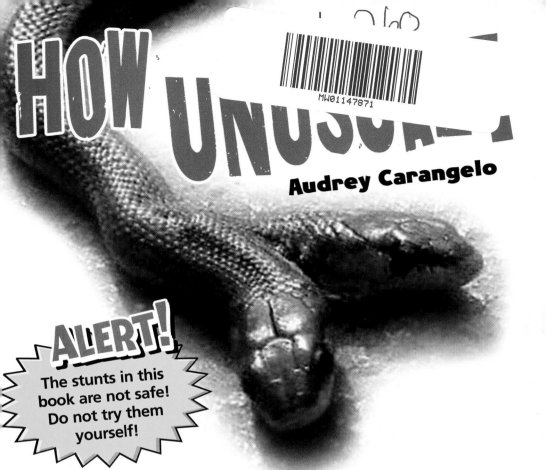

HOW UNUSUAL?

Audrey Carangelo

ALERT!

The stunts in this book are not safe! Do not try them yourself!

PHOTO CREDITS Cover: © Dani Cardona/Reuters; title page: © Dani Cardona/Reuters; p. 2: © Dani Cardona/Reuters; p. 3: © 2004 Ripley Entertainment Inc.; p. 4: © Javier Galeano/AP/Wide World Photos; p. 5: © 2004 Ripley Entertainment Inc.; p. 6: © 2004 Ripley Entertainment Inc.; p. 7: © 2004 Ripley Entertainment Inc.; p. 8: © 2004 Ripley Entertainment Inc.; p. 9: © Ron Cohn, The Gorilla Foundation, Koko.org; p. 10: © Lisa Carpenter; p. 11: © 2004 Ripley Entertainment Inc.; p. 12: © Bettmann/Corbis; p. 13 © The Natural History Museum, London; p. 14: © 2004 Ripley Entertainment Inc.; p. 15: © Digital Vision; p. 16: © 2004 Ripley Entertainment Inc.

ISBN 0-439-75712-6

SCHOLASTIC, SCHOLASTIC FX BOOKS, and associated logos and designs are trademarks and/or registered trademarks of Scholastic Inc.

LEXILE is a registered trademark of MetaMetrics, Inc.

5 6 7 8 9 10   40   14 13 12 11 10

SCHOLASTIC INC.

New York Toronto London Auckland Sydney Mexico City
New Delhi Hong Kong Buenos Aires

Are you sick of the dull? Are you bored with the boring? Then this book is for you! It tells about some funky animals. You will also see people with wacky skills. They may impress you!

We're not bluffing.

This snake has two heads!

I wonder if they get along.

This man grips pencils with his hands. He also grips them with his feet!

It looks simple. But that's just because he's such a champ. He can sketch four pictures at once!

Are your shoes too <u>snug</u>?
Try this one on! <u>This</u>
man makes <u>fun</u> shoes for
clowns. He wanted to <u>set</u>
a world record. So he made
the world's longest shoe.

The shoe is over nine
feet long. It must be tough
<u>lugging</u> it like <u>that</u>!

Give this snapshot a close look. Can you <u>trust</u> what you see?

It's true! <u>This</u> man can twist his head <u>until</u> it's backward! What a talent! <u>That</u> <u>must</u> hurt his <u>neck</u>.

Don't try <u>this</u> at home!

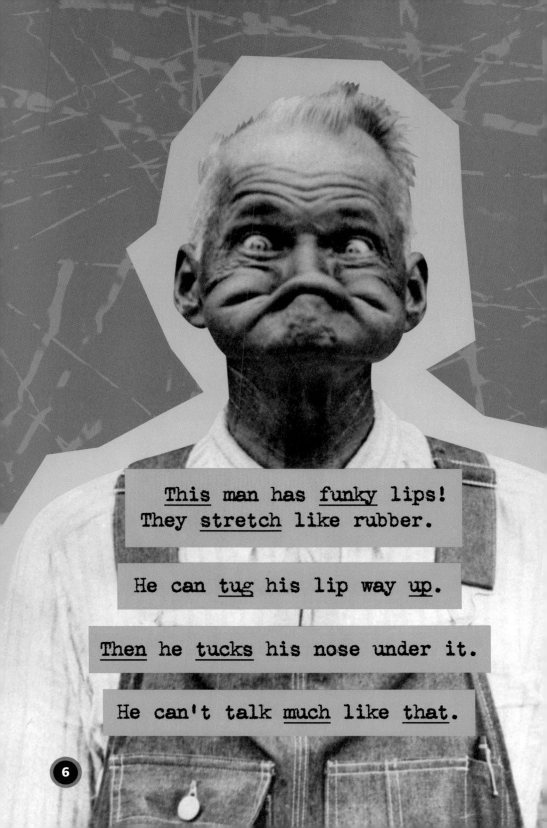

This man has <u>funky</u> lips! They <u>stretch</u> like rubber.

He can <u>tug</u> his lip way <u>up</u>.

<u>Then</u> he <u>tucks</u> his nose under it.

He can't talk <u>much</u> like <u>that</u>.

Don't try <u>this</u> <u>stunt</u> yourself! <u>This</u> man can lift three mowers. He <u>rests</u> <u>them</u> on his chin!

But can he <u>cut</u> the grass <u>that</u> way? Would you <u>trust</u> him not to drop one on your <u>skull</u>?

If we tried <u>this</u>, we'd get <u>stung</u>. But <u>this</u> man is a bee expert. He <u>spends</u> <u>much</u> of his time with bees. Sometimes, he <u>lets</u> bees <u>settle</u> on his chin. He <u>trusts</u> <u>that</u> he won't get <u>stung</u>.

This is Koko.

She paints stuff for fun.

She uses lots of colors.

She selects them herself.

Does she do a good job? You be the judge.

This is not a dog. It is a horse. But just like some dogs, it helps blind people. Like lots of dogs, the horse lives in a house!

Check out his feet! His tennis shoes stop him from slipping!

Lots of monkeys swing
from trees in the <u>jungle</u>.

But <u>this</u> monkey is <u>nuts</u> about water.

He <u>jumps</u> on his skis.

<u>Then</u> he <u>gets</u> pulled across the pond.

Do you <u>think</u> he has more
<u>fun</u> <u>than</u> other monkeys?

Do the <u>math</u>.

These nails are <u>ultra-long</u>!

In fact, they <u>stretch</u> over six inches!

Are they <u>press-on</u> nails?
No! They are real!

Is <u>this</u> a monster <u>bug</u>?
No. It's the biggest
spider on the planet.
   Do you know what it
eats for <u>lunch</u>? Sometimes,
it <u>munches</u> on a bird!

This man made a jumbo ball
of yarn. Then he rolled it
onto his grass. That's a
big job! He must think he's
really buff!

<u>This</u> dog has really long ears! They <u>must</u> flap in the wind. Do you <u>think</u> he trips on <u>them</u>? Does <u>stuff</u> get <u>stuck</u> on <u>them</u> when he eats?

Is <u>that</u> the world's biggest hand?
No, it is the littlest pool table.

It really works! But it is very little.

A big <u>bug</u> could knock
it over with one <u>bump</u>.

What do you think of the <u>stuff</u>
in this book? Did it <u>puzzle</u> you?
Did it make you grin?